BLACK HISTORY TREASURE CHEST
With the Sarah Mae Flemming's Story

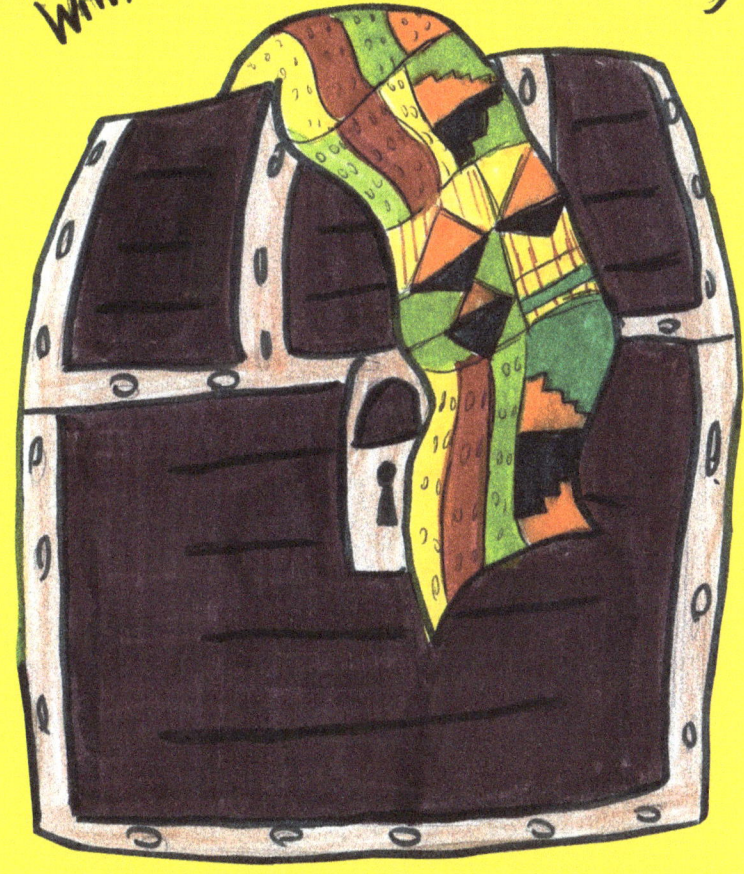

Author R.S. Roberson

Illustrator Christon K. Simons

GOLD?? SILVER?? LEGACIES???

Copyright © 2023 Rosetta Smoot Roberson.

All rights reserved. No part of this book may be used or reproduced by any means, graphic, electronic, or mechanical, including photocopying, recording, taping or by any information storage retrieval system without the written permission of the author except in the case of brief quotations embodied in critical articles and reviews.

Uriel Press books may be ordered through booksellers or by contacting:

Uriel Press
1663 Liberty Drive
Bloomington, IN 47403
www.urielpress.com
844-752-3114

Because of the dynamic nature of the Internet, any web addresses or links contained in this book may have changed since publication and may no longer be valid. The views expressed in this work are solely those of the author and do not necessarily reflect the views of the publisher, and the publisher hereby disclaims any responsibility for them.

Any people depicted in stock imagery provided by Getty Images are models, and such images are being used for illustrative purposes only. Certain stock imagery © Getty Images.

ISBN: 979-8-8861-2023-3 (sc)
ISBN: 979-8-8861-2024-0 (e)

Library of Congress Control Number: 2023918637

Print information available on the last page.

Urial Press rev. date: 11/06/2023

This book is dedicated to all unknown as well as the known persons who used their God-given courage to stand for social justice while being seeds for the civil right movement.

Today, Kapara is going to visit her great aunt Rosena for the weekend. She is very excited about her visit because Aunt Rosena is a very good cook. She plays cards, board games, and tells the funniest jokes. She is a great storyteller too. Kapara is of a mixed heritage - African American and Caucasian.

"Going to Aunt Rosena's house is like visiting a museum," Kapara told her mom. "Yes, she does have some unusual and strange items," chuckled Mom.

The drive to Aunt Rosena is a twenty-mile ride. Kapara was on her phone during the trip. "Mom, do you think Aunt Rosena has gotten a computer by now?" asked Kapara. "Maybe," said Mom. "There's that old Underwood typewriter on the shelf."

They both laughed.

"Well, we are here," said Mom.

Aunt Rosena met them at the door. "Welcome," she said while giving them both a tight hug.

Mom reminded Aunt Rosena that she would return to get Kapara on Sunday evening.

Mom kissed them both and said "Bye now."

As Kapara went to the guest room, she looked all around to spot anything she hadn't seen before. After placing her things in the room,

she went into the family room. She noticed the old typewriter was in its place. There was a huge trunk below the shelf. It was shaped like a treasure chest. An African print throw was across it.

"That's new," Kapara said.

"It's my Black History treasure chest child, remarked Aunt Rosena, and you may look inside of it."

Inside the trunk were magazines: Ebony, Look, Essence, newspapers, and African print post cards. Magazine covers featured Rosa Parks, Coretta Scott King, Barack Obama, Malcolm X, Nelson Mandela, and others. Newspapers headlines were about a church bombing in Alabama and the forgotten hero-story of Sarah Mae Flemming.

Kapara took a decorative pillow, placed it under her head, stretched out on the floor, and began to read.

Finally, she sat up and said, "I never heard of Sarah Mae Flemming."

"Well, her story is similar to Rosa Parks' story," declared Aunt Rosena. "That article opened many eyes in the community," she went on to say.

The article reported that Sarah rode to and from work on a segregated city bus in Columbia, SC. She was ordered to give up her seat for a white passenger and leave from the back door. The bus driver even assaulted her by hitting her in her stomach. Her legal battle went to federal court twice, but was thrown out.

"In recent years, Sarah Mae Flemming has been acknowledged in the 2008 SC African American History calendar (March), by a name plate attached to Columbia city Main street sign, the Center for Civil Rights History and Research, a mural of her and the SCEG Bus, documentaries in University of SC African American museum, and large billboards of her were positioned along a major state highway," reported Aunt Rosena. "You know what, I have a laptop and you can search for the documentary, *Before Rosa*," said Aunt Rosena. Aunt Rosena got her laptop from under her old Underwood typewriter and handed it to Kapara.

"Wow, Sarah Mae Flemming, you are no longer unknown to me," said Kapara.

As Kapara searched for information about Sarah Mae, she came across an article about a traveling civil rights history exhibit with traveling trunks.

"Aunt Rosena, the Justice for All exhibit has traveling trunks. Do you want your trunk to travel?" asked Kapara.

"No thanks," said Aunt Rosena.

Kapara continues to read and up pops more recent information. It reads that the city of Columbia, Town of Eastover, and Richland County have declared June 22 as Sarah Mae Flemming Day.

She later found that Sarah Mae is on display in the International African American Museum in Charleston, S.C.

Kapara placed her hands at waist and said, "Wow!"

Kapara found this timeline from her reading.

Sarah Mae Flemming vs SCEG

June 22, 1954 - Sarah is ordered to move from a seat on the bus.

July 21, 1954 - Attorney Wittenberg filed federal lawsuit on Sarah's behalf.

Feb. 16, 1955 - Judge Timmerman dismissed the case declaring city buses didn't fall under Brown vs. Board of Education.

July 14, 1955 - Circuit appeals court reversed Timmerman decision.
June 12, 1956 - Flemming's first jury trial begins in Columbia.

June 13, 1956 - Timmerman cuts the trial short and dismissed the case a second time.

Nov. 29, 1956 - Appeals court ruled again in Flemming's favor and sends the case back to Timmerman for trial.

June 11, 1957 - Columbia jury decides SCE&G owes nothing to Flemming

Source: The STATE (March 30, 2003)

Sarah Mae Flemming was a daughter, sister, wife, mother, and an unsung hero. She was a member of Goodwill Baptist Church of Eastover, S.C. Her ancestors no doubt worked as slaves on the Goodwill Plantation. The seed of indignity she endured helped civil rights leaders build a strong case for Rosa Parks and the desegregation of bus transportation.

To learn more Google, Sarah Mae Flemming.

THANK YOU

Christon K. Simons

Mrs. Anna S. Merchant

Mrs. Yvonne Flemming

Mrs. Wanda Brown Hall